Teen Practical Life Skills Workbook

Facilitator Reproducible Self-Assessments, Exercises & Educational Handouts

Ester A. Leutenberg

John J. Liptak, EdD

Illustrated by

Amy L. Brodsky, LISW-S

wholeperson
Stress & Wellness Publishers
Duluth, Minnesota

Whole Person
101 West 2ⁿᵈ St., Suite 203
Duluth, MN 55802-1908

800-247-6789

books@wholeperson.com
www.wholeperson.com

Teen Practical Life Skills Workbook
Facilitator Reproducible Self-Assessments,
Exercises & Educational Handouts

Printed in the United States of America

10 9 8 7 6 5 4 3 2 1

Editorial Director: Carlene Sippola
Art Director: Joy Morgan Dey

Library of Congress Control Number:2012950496
ISBN: 978-1-57025-267-9

Using This Book *(For the professional)*

One important task of teens is learning practical life skills, critical for personal and professional success. Research indicates that life skills intelligence is as important as a teen's intelligence quotient (IQ) and emotional intelligence. Teens depend on effective life skills every day. With these skills they create a successful quality of life as they grow their inner resources.

Effective practical life skills help teens take charge and manage their lives in an increasingly complex society. Life skills can help them manage change and work effectively with their environments, their peers and other adults. The purpose of this workbook is to help teens develop the critical life skills that will assist them in meeting the demands of everyday life in a safe, mature and responsible manner.

The most important reason life skills intelligence is of such high importance is that, unlike the knowledge measured by traditional IQ tests, life skills can be learned and refined so that one can lead a successful, satisfying and productive life. *A person's life skills IQ is a composite of many other types of intelligence:

- **Physical Intelligence** – focus on nutritional practices; interest in regular exercise; consistent and adequate sleep; ability to say NO to drugs and alcohol; responsibility for personal healthy habits; and respect for one's own body.

- **Mental Intelligence** – focus on the ability to engage in clear thinking and recall of information, with minimal interference from emotional baggage; ability to think independently and critically; possession of basic reasoning skills; interest in new ideas; knowledge of one's cultural heritage as well as others; ability to use good common sense in everyday life; and interest in lifelong learning.

- **Job, Volunteer and School Intelligence** – focus on maximizing one's own skills and abilities; ability to maintain a sense of control over the demands of school, volunteering and ultimately the workplace; responsible money management; power to balance time and energy spent at school, job, volunteering, friends, family and leisure; knowledge of one's interests, values, and personality; knowledge of procedures and expectations in each of these areas; and knowledge of strengths as well as areas of growth and improvement.

- **Emotional Intelligence** – focus on awareness of one's emotions; ability to maintain an even emotional state with appropriate emotional responses in reaction to any event; ability to maintain control over emotional states; ability to understand one's feelings; and ability to be aware and care about others' feelings.

- **Social Intelligence** – focus on sharing, friendship, and membership in groups; ability to practice active listening and empathy; interest in caring for others; awareness of social norms and cues; and willingness to caring and showing commitment to the common good of all people, community and the world.

- **Spiritual Intelligence** – focus on issues of meaning, values and purpose; interest in the importance of and search for clarity; search for greater meaning in life; commitment to faith and optimism; interest in developing the inner self and identifying purpose to life; and ability to see the whole picture, not just isolated events.

*Liptak, J.J. (2007). *Life Skills IQ Test*. New York: Penguin Publishing.

(Continued on the next page)

Using This Book *(For the professional, continued)*

The *Teen Practical Life Skills Workbook* contains five separate sections to help participants learn more about themselves and the competencies they possess in many life skills areas. Participants will learn about the importance of life skills in their daily lives. They will complete assessments and activities to keep them become better managers of life and to assist their development of greater life skills.

The sections of this book are:

1) **PROBLEM-SOLVING STYLE SCALE** helps teens understand how they attempt to solve problems, and provides instruction to improve their problem-solving skills.

2) **MONEY MANAGEMENT STYLE SCALE** helps teens to identify their style in managing money, and provides instruction for capable money management.

3) **TIME MANAGEMENT SKILLS SCALE** helps teens identify how efficient they are at managing their time, and provides instruction for better time management.

4) **SELF-AWARENESS SCALE** helps teens identify their level of self-awareness related to their emotions, self-confidence and self-assessment.

5) **PERSONAL CHANGE SCALE** helps teens identify the changes they are experiencing in their lives, and provides instruction for managing change.

By combining reflective assessment and journaling, participants will be exposed to a powerful method of verbalizing and writing to reflect on and solve problems. Participants will become more aware of the strength and areas for growth and improvements of their daily life skills.

Preparation for using the assessments and activities in this book is important. The authors suggest that prior to administering any of the assessments in this book, you complete them yourself. This will familiarize you with the format of the assessments, the scoring directions, the interpretation guides and the journaling activities. Although the assessments are designed to be self-administered, scored and interpreted, this familiarity will help prepare facilitators to answer participants' questions about the assessments.

Use Name Codes for Confidentiality

Confidentiality is a term for any action that preserves the privacy of other people. Because teens completing the activities in this workbook might be asked to answer assessment items and to journal about and explore their relationships, you will need to discuss confidentiality before you begin using the materials in this workbook. Maintaining confidentiality is important as it shows respect for others and allows participants to explore their feelings without hurting anyone's feelings or fearing gossip, harm or retribution.

In order to maintain confidentiality, explain to the participants that they need to assign a name code for each person they write about as they complete the various activities in the workbook. For example, a friend named Joey who enjoys going to hockey games might be titled JLHG (Joey Loves Hockey Games) for a particular exercise. In order to protect their friends' identities, they may not use people's actual names or initials, just name codes.

The Assessments, Journaling Activities and Educational Handouts

The Assessments, Journaling Activities, and Educational Handouts in the *Teen Practical Life Skills Workbook* are reproducible and ready to be photocopied for participants' use. Assessments contained in this book focus on self-reported data and can be used by psychologists, counselors, therapists, teachers and career consultants. Accuracy and usefulness of the information provided is dependent on the truthful information that each participant provides through self-examination. By being honest, participants help themselves to learn about unproductive and ineffective patterns, and to uncover information that might be keeping them from being as happy and/or as successful as they might be.

An assessment instrument can provide participants with valuable information about themselves; however, it cannot measure or identify everything about them. The purpose of an assessment is not to pigeon-hole certain characteristics, but rather to allow participants to explore all of their characteristics. This book contains self-assessments, not tests. Tests measure knowledge or whether something is right or wrong. For the assessments in this book, there are no right or wrong answers. These assessments ask for personal opinions or attitudes about a topic of importance in the participant's career and life.

When administering assessments in this workbook, remember that the items are generically written so that they will be applicable to a wide variety of teens but will not account for every possible variable for every teen. Use them to help participants identify possible negative themes in their lives and find ways to break the hold that these patterns and their effects have.

Advise the teens taking the assessments that they should not spend too much time trying to analyze the content of the questions; their initial response will most likely be true. Regardless of individual scores, encourage teens to talk about their findings and their feelings pertaining to what they have discovered about themselves. Talking about and working on practical life skills will improve their quality of life as well as assist them in developing the skills to self-access throughout life. These exercises can be used by group facilitators working with any teens who want to strengthen their overall wellness.

A particular score on any assessment does not guarantee a participant's level of life skills. Use discretion when using any of the information or feedback provided in this workbook. The use of these assessments should not be substituted for consultation and wellness planning with a health care professional.

Thanks to the following professionals whose input into this book has been so valuable!

Carol Butler, MS Ed, RN, C
Annette Damien, MS,PPS
Jay Leutenberg
Kathy Liptak, Ed.D.
Eileen Regen, M.Ed., CJE

Layout of the Book

The *Teen Practical Life Skills Workbook* is designed to be used either independently or as part of an integrated curriculum. You may administer one of the assessments and the journaling exercises to an individual or a group with whom you are working, or you may administer a number of the assessments over one or more days.

This book Includes the following reproducible pages in the first five sections:

- **Assessment Instruments** – Self-assessment inventories with scoring directions and interpretation materials. Group facilitators can choose one or more of the activities relevant to their participants.

- **Activity Handouts** – Practical questions and activities that prompt self-reflection and promote self-understanding. These questions and activities foster introspection and promote pro-social behaviors.

- **Quotations** – Quotations are used in each section to provide insight and promote reflection. Participants will be asked to select one or more of the quotations and journal about what the quotations mean to them.

- **Reflective Questions for Journaling** – Self-exploration activities and journaling exercises specific to each assessment to enhance self-discovery, learning, and healing.

- **Educational Handouts** – Handouts designed to enhance instruction can be used individually or in groups to promote a positive responsibility for safety at home, in the classroom, and in the community. They can be distributed, scanned and converted into masters for overheads or transparencies, projected or written on boards and/or discussed.

Who Should Use This Program?

This book has been designed as a practical tool for helping professionals, such as therapists, school counselors, psychologists, guidance counselors, teachers, group leaders, etc. Depending on the role of the professional using the *Teen Practical Life Skills Workbook* and the specific group's needs, these sections can be used individually or combined for a more comprehensive approach.

Why Use Self-Assessments?

Self-assessments are important in responding to various teen life skills issues because they help participants to engage in these ways:

- Become aware of the primary motivators that guide their behavior.
- Explore and learn to "let go" of troublesome habits and behavioral patterns.
- Explore the effects of unconscious childhood messages.
- Gain insight and "a wake-up call" for behavioral change.
- Focus their thinking on behavioral goals for change.
- Uncover resources they possess that can help them to cope better with safety.
- Explore their personal characteristics without judgment.
- Be fully aware of their strengths and areas for growth.

Because the assessments are presented in a straightforward and easy-to-use format, individuals can self-administer, score and interpret each assessment at their own pace.

Teen Introduction

Learning powerful skills that you can use throughout various stages of your life is essential for your personal development. These skills will help you to develop a sense of individualism, succeed both in school and in the workplace, and develop practical abilities to improve your relationships. Life skills are those skills that you take for granted, such as cleverly managing your money and your time, solving problems that you encounter, dealing with change that occurs in your life, and becoming more self-aware.

Life skills practice allows you to develop skills needed to deal in a smart way with the personal challenges and changes that occur in your life, and which will continue to help you as an adult. Lack of powerful life skills, whether they are direct in helping you achieve your goals, or not, have a tendency to keep repeating themselves if they are left unexamined. That is the reason many people go through life using ineffective life skills over and over again and expecting different results each time. Once you have identified your negative patterns and skills, you will have the power to alter them so that you begin to experience positive results as you build your repertoire of positive and strong life skills.

Life skills training can help you to begin taking responsibility for managing your own life by mastering the skills that will help you to become the best person you can be and realize your full potential. Successful life skills allow you to deal with the inevitable setbacks and problems you will encounter in life. This book, the *Teen Practical Life Skills Workbook*, is designed to help you learn more about yourself, identify your effective and ineffective life skills, and find better ways to use these skills to positively adapt to and deal with the unique challenges in your life.

Confidentiality

You will be asked to respond to assessments and exercises, and to journal about some experiences in your life. Everyone has the right to confidentiality, and you need to honor the right of everyone's privacy. Think about it this way – you would not want someone writing things about you that other people could read. Your friends feel this way also.

In order to maintain the confidentiality of your friends, assign people code names based on things you know about them. For example, a friend named Sherry who loves to wear purple might be coded as SWP (Sherry Wears Purple). **Do not use any person's actual name when you are listing people – use only name codes.**

Teen Practical Life Skills Workbook
TABLE OF CONTENTS

TABLE OF CONTENTS

TABLE OF CONTENTS

SECTION I:
Problem-Solving Style Scale

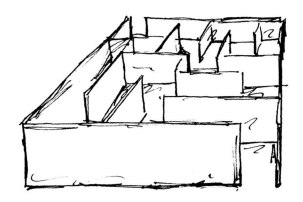

Name_____

Date_____

Problem-Solving Style Scale
Directions

Problems occur in the lives of all people. Some problems are large and some are small. The ability to solve problems determines how satisfied you will be in many aspects of your life. By being able to solve problems effectively, you will live a healthier and less stressful life. Different people have different approaches to solving problems and the approach that you use is largely based on your own personality. The *Problem-Solving Style Scale* is designed to help you understand how you attempt to solve problems and guide you to additional skills in effective problem solving.

In the following example, the circled 1 indicates the statement is not at all descriptive of the person completing the inventory:

Please answer the following statements based on a recent problem you solved.

Describe the problem:

EXAMPLE: I saw someone being bullied and I told a trusted adult.

Read each of the statements and decide how descriptive the statement is of your recent problem. Circle the number of your response of each statement.

	A Lot Like Me	Somewhat Like Me	A Little Like Me	Not Like Me
1. When I solved this problem . . .				
I focused on what really happened to cause the problem	4	3	2	(1)

This is not a test and there are no right or wrong answers. Do not spend too much time thinking about your answers. Your initial response will likely be the most true for you. Be sure to respond to every statement.

(Turn to the next page and begin)

Problem-Solving Style Scale

Please answer the following statements based on a recent problem you solved

Describe the problem:

_____

	A Lot Like Me	Somewhat Like Me	A Little Like Me	Not Like Me
1. When I solved this problem . . .				
I focused on what really happened to cause the problem	4	3	2	1
I paid attention to specifics and details	4	3	2	1
I looked for the pros and cons	4	3	2	1
I tried to find a practical solution to the problem	4	3	2	1
I viewed the problem realistically	4	3	2	1
I relied on experience and standard ways to solve it	4	3	2	1
I gathered as many facts as possible	4	3	2	1

TOTAL #1 = _____

	A Lot Like Me	Somewhat Like Me	A Little Like Me	Not Like Me
2. When I solved this problem . . .				
I reacted to my gut feelings	4	3	2	1
I looked at the big picture, not small details	4	3	2	1
I did what felt right	4	3	2	1
I tried to be creative	4	3	2	1
I relied on internal signals about what feels right	4	3	2	1
I thought about how this will affect everyone involved	4	3	2	1
I valued insights over facts	4	3	2	1

TOTAL #2 = _____

(Continued on the next page)

Problem-Solving Style Scale *(Continued)*

3. When I solved this problem . . .

	A Lot Like Me	Somewhat Like Me	A Little Like Me	Not Like Me
I looked at it logically	4	3	2	1
I analyzed the facts and put them in order	4	3	2	1
I wanted to find the one right answer	4	3	2	1
I thought about what one of my role models would do	4	3	2	1
I paid attention to all details of the problem	4	3	2	1
I did not get overly emotional	4	3	2	1
I concentrated on the problem, not the outcome	4	3	2	1

TOTAL #3 = _____

4. When I solved this problem . . .

	A Lot Like Me	Somewhat Like Me	A Little Like Me	Not Like Me
I tried to be helpful in the best possible way	4	3	2	1
I concerned myself about the other people involved	4	3	2	1
I tried to sense how others felt about my solution	4	3	2	1
I wanted the best solution for everyone involved	4	3	2	1
I let my emotions be part of the process	4	3	2	1
I tried to work out a solution best for everyone	4	3	2	1
I trusted my feelings about the situation	4	3	2	1

TOTAL #4 = _____

(Go to the Scoring Directions on the next page)

Problem-Solving Style Scale
Scoring Directions

The Problem-Solving Style Scale is designed to measure the way you solve problems. For each of the four sections, add the scores you circled for each of the items. Put that total on the line marked "Total" at the end of each section.

Then, transfer your totals to the spaces below:

Problem-Solving Style

1. TOTAL = _____	Practical Thinking
2. TOTAL = _____	Intuitive Thinking
3. TOTAL = _____	Logical Thinking
4. TOTAL = _____	Social Sensitive Thinking

Profile Interpretation

Individual Scales Scores	Result	Indications
Scores from 22 to 28	high	Scores from 22 to 28 on any single scale indicate that you have many of the characteristics of people with that particular problem-solving style.
Scores from 14 to 21	moderate	Scores from 14 to 21 on any single scale indicate that you have some of the characteristics of people with that particular problem-solving style.
Scores from 7 to 13	low	Scores from 7 to 13 on any single scale indicate that you do not have many of the characteristics of people with that particular problem-solving style.

Go to the next page to learn more about the various problem-solving styles.

For scales which you scored in the **Moderate** or **High** range, find the descriptions on the pages that follow. Then, read the description and complete the exercises that are included. No matter how you scored, low, moderate or high, you will benefit from **every one of these exercises.**

In the following exercises, remember to use Name Codes for the people you describe.

Problem-Solving Style Scale

Profile Scale Descriptions #1 – Practical Thinking

A PRACTICAL THINKING Problem-Solving Style is one in which you take in information that is clear and real. You want to know what is happening in the situation. You notice what is going on around you, especially the practical realities and facts. You may overlook recurring themes, focusing instead on the concrete issues involved in the situation. You rely on and trust your previous experience in dealing with similar problems.

If this is your style, place a check in the box by the characteristics that sound like you:

- ❏ You stick with it until you find a solution to a problem.
- ❏ You focus on what is really happening.
- ❏ You trust your experience from previous problem situations.
- ❏ You trust facts rather than other people.
- ❏ You are perceptive.
- ❏ You are able to remember specific facts about the problem.
- ❏ You understand ideas through practical applications.
- ❏ You carefully work toward conclusions.

Write about a time when the Practical Thinking Problem-Solving Style worked well for you.

_____

_____

_____

_____

_____

Write about a time when the Practical Thinking Problem-Solving Style did NOT work.

_____

_____

_____

_____

_____

Problem-Solving Style Scale
Profile Scale Descriptions #2 – Intuitive Thinking

An INTUITIVE THINKING Problem-Solving Style is one in which you solve problems based on gut-level reactions. You tend to rely on your internal signals. You identify and choose a solution based on what you feel is the best possible solution for everyone involved. You do not spend a lot of time collecting facts and gathering information before you decide on a solution. This style can be useful when factual data is not available. It is important not to substitute intuition for gathering needed information to solve the problem. You often solve problems based on hunches or your *sixth-sense* about the problem situation.

If this is your style, place a check in the box by the characteristics that sounds like you:

- ❏ You consider the future.
- ❏ You communicate creatively.
- ❏ You develop imaginative solutions to problems.
- ❏ You reach solutions quickly, based on your hunches.
- ❏ You look for similarities in other problems you have needed to solve.
- ❏ You need the problem to make sense to you.
- ❏ You are able to see new possibilities.
- ❏ You see the big picture.

Write about a time when the Intuitive Thinking Problem-Solving Style worked well for you.

_____

_____

_____

_____

Write a time when the Intuitive Thinking Problem-Solving Style did NOT work.

_____

_____

_____

_____

Problem-Solving Style Scale

Profile Scale Descriptions #3 – Logical Thinking

A LOGICAL THINKING Problem-Solving Style involves the exploration of the problem and the effects of your environment. Using this style, you identify the problem that has occurred, explore alternatives in solving the problem, and develop a plan for solving the problem based on information. You carefully weigh the costs and benefits of the various ways to solve the problem. You gather and consider additional information about alternatives and the possible consequences of each alternative. The ultimate solution you find to the problem is based on a logical problem-solving approach.

If this is your style, place a check in the box by the characteristics that sound like you:

❏ You are analytical.

❏ You look for possible solutions to problems.

❏ You rely on your good judgment.

❏ You are reasonable.

❏ You have good common sense.

❏ You want everyone to be treated equally.

❏ You develop solutions and then choose the best options.

❏ You remove yourself emotionally from the situation.

Write about a time when the Logical Thinking Problem-Solving Style worked well for you.

_____

_____

_____

_____

Write about a time when the Logical Thinking Problem-Solving Style did NOT work.

_____

_____

_____

_____

Problem-Solving Style Scale

Profile Scale Descriptions #4 – Social Sensitive Thinking

A SOCIAL SENSITIVE THINKING Problem-Solving Style is one in which you want to find the best answer for all people involved (focusing primarily on their emotions and values, and you are most comfortable when they add emotion to the problem situation.) You depend on what has been successful for you in the past, rather than focusing on the facts of this new issue. You try to put yourself in the other person's place so that you can identify with the person. You will solve problems based on your value system that respects other people in a situation. You are caring and want to support everyone involved in the problem. This indicates a high level of interpersonal skills.

If this is your style, place a check in the box by the characteristics that sound like you:

❏ You are considerate to others in the situation.

❏ You are guided by your own personal issues.

❏ You are compassionate.

❏ You assess the impact of the problem on other people.

❏ You want everyone to be satisfied in the situation.

❏ Others call you caring and/or compassionate.

❏ You always try to treat others fairly.

❏ You believe that positive interactions are important in solving problems.

Write about a time when the Social Sensitive Thinking Problem-Solving Style worked well for you.

_____

_____

_____

_____

Write about a time when the Social Sensitive Thinking Problem-Solving Style did NOT work.

_____

_____

_____

_____

Becoming a Skillful Problem Solver

Look back at some of the problems you have solved in the past. Problems may have dealt with your relationships, home-life, education or your job. List these problems and write down how you approached a solution to each pattern that you noticed.

Problems I Have Solved

Example of when I could have used the PRACTICAL THINKING style to solve a problem better than I solved it:

_____

_____

_____

_____

Example of when I could have used the INTUITIVE THINKING style to solve a problem better than I solved it:

_____

_____

_____

_____

Example of when I could have used the LOGICAL THINKING style to solve a problem better than I solved it:

_____

_____

_____

_____

Example of when I could have used the SOCIAL SENSITIVE THINKING style to solve a problem better than I solved it:

_____

_____

_____

_____

The Problem-Solving Process
OUTLINE (page 1)

There is no simple step-by-step process that will guarantee you a solution to every problem you encounter in your life. The problem-solving process is a search for, and implementation of, the best possible solution for a specific problem. As a problem solver, you will develop your own method for solving problems. One of the best methods for doing this is to try to use the most effective aspects of the four different styles. The following is an outline of how to integrate the four styles in the problem-solving process.

Write the problem you used to answer the statements in the Problem-Solving Style Scale.

_____

Step 1 – Define the problem by using **Practical Thinking** characteristics to see the problem situation as it really is. You can do so by answering some of the following questions:

- What or who caused the problem?_____
- Where did it happen?_____
- What happened?_____
- When did it happen? _____
- With whom did it happen? _____
- Why did it happen? _____
- What was your part in the situation?_____
- What was resolved?_____

Step 2 – Consider the possibilities using **Intuitive Thinking** characteristics to brainstorm all possible solutions to the problem. You can do so by answering some of the following questions:

- What other ways did you look at the problem? _____
- What did you learn by information you gathered? _____
- What were the connections to the bigger picture? _____
- How did the other people fit into this picture?_____
- What did you think caused the problem?_____
- What were some possible ways to approach the problem? _____

(Continued on the next page)

The Problem-Solving Process
OUTLINE (page 2)

Step 3 – Weigh the consequences of courses of action to resolve the problem using **Logical Thinking** characteristics. You can do so by answering some of the following questions:

- What were the pros of each option? _____

- What were the cons of each option? _____

- What do you think would have been the outcomes of each option? _____

- What was the result for each person involved?_____

Step 4 – Weigh the alternatives to each course of action using **Social Sensitive Thinking** characteristics. You can do so by answering some of the following questions:

- How did each alternative fit with your values? _____

- How were the other people involved in the situation affected?_____

- How did each alternative help everyone involved? _____

- How did each alternative enhance positive interactions? _____

Step 5 – Decide which aspects of Steps 1 – 4 will be most effective in solving this problem.

_____

Step 6 – Act on your decision.

Step 7 – Evaluate whether the problem was resolved successfully. _____

_____

_____

Complete the following four Problem Solving activity pages.

Problem-Solving Activity (page 1)

Identify a major problem you are currently facing. _____

_____

Complete this 4-page activity that will guide you through the appreciation of the problem-solving process.

Step 1 – Define the problem by using PRACTICAL THINKING characteristics to see the problem situation as it really is. You can do so by answering some of the following questions:

What is causing the problem?

_____

_____

Where is it happening?

_____

_____

What happened?

_____

_____

When did it start?

_____

_____

Who is involved?

_____

_____

Why is it happening?

_____

_____

What is your part in the situation?

_____

_____

What has already been tried to resolve the situation?

_____

Problem-Solving Activity (page 2)

Step 2 – Consider the possibilities using INTUITIVE THINKING characteristics to brainstorm all possible solutions to the problem. You can do so by answering some of the following questions:

What other ways can you look at the problem?

_____

_____

_____

What does the information that you have gathered suggest to you?

_____

_____

_____

What are the connections to the bigger picture?

_____

_____

_____

How do the other people fit into this picture?

_____

_____

_____

What do you think is causing the problem?

_____

_____

_____

What are some possible ways to approach the problem?

_____

_____

_____

Problem-Solving Activity (page 3)

Step 3 – Weigh the consequences of courses of action to resolve the problem using LOGICAL THINKING characteristics. You can do so by answering some of the following questions:

What are the pros of each option?

_____

_____

_____

_____

_____

What are the cons of each option?

_____

_____

_____

_____

_____

What are the possible outcomes of each option?

_____

_____

_____

_____

_____

How would each option affect each person involved?

_____

_____

_____

_____

_____

Problem-Solving Activity (page 4)

Step 4 – Weigh the alternatives to each course of action using SOCIAL SENSITIVE THINKING characteristics. You can do so by answering some of the following questions:

How does each alternative fit with my values?

_____

_____

How will the other people involved in the situation be affected?

_____

_____

How will each alternative contribute to harmony for all people involved?

_____

_____

How will each alternative enhance positive interactions?

_____

_____

Step 5 – Decide which parts of Steps 1 – 4 will be most effective in solving this problem. _____

_____

Step 6 – Make a final decision.

_____

Step 7 – Act on your decision. What do you need to do to begin?

_____

_____

Step 8 – LATER, answer . . . How was the problem resolved? _____

_____

My Problems

What types of problems do you encounter the most?
(conflicts with friends, time and money management, family issues, communications, etc.)

_____

_____

_____

_____

_____

_____

_____

_____

_____

_____

_____

_____

How do these problems affect your life?

_____

_____

_____

_____

_____

_____

_____

_____

_____

_____

_____

_____

Problem-Solving

With whom do you have most of your problems?

_____

_____

_____

_____

_____

_____

_____

_____

_____

_____

_____

What parts of the other problem-solving styles do you want to add into your own style?

_____

_____

_____

_____

_____

_____

_____

_____

_____

_____

_____

_____

Teen Problems Today

In the following list are just some of the problems teens face:

- Abuse
- Alcohol and drug-using parents
- Alternative lifestyle acceptance
- Anxiety
- Authority figures
- Body issues
- Bullying
- Cheating
- Cultural acceptance
- Cyber Bullying
- Date rape
- Dating
- Depression
- Deciding on a career
- Discrimination
- Drinking
- Drugs
- Family
- Finances
- Further education
- Gambling
- Gang activity
- Grades

- Illegal actions
- Low self-esteem
- Mental health
- Mixed family
- Money matters
- Obesity
- Peer pressure
- Performing well in school
- Pregnancy
- Prejudicing
- Relationships
- Risky Behavior
- Self-Image
- Self-Injury
- Sexually transmitted diseases
- Shoplifting
- Stress
- Suicide
- Teasing
- Unsafe driving
- Unstable home life
- Violence at home
- Youth violence

Other Ways to Solve Problems

Divide

Break problems into smaller, solvable problems.

Brainstorm

List all of the possible solutions, no matter how outrageous they seem.

Test

Think of possible solutions to the problem and then try to predict the final outcome.

Research

Get valid information from trusted people and *reliable* sources on the internet.

Past Experience

Remember similar problems, how you solved them and what worked. Ask others what worked for them in similar situations.

Trial-and-error

Create and implement solutions, then see if they work.

Stop focusing on the problem

When your mind is allowed to focus on other things, the solution may become obvious.

SECTION II:

Money Management Style Scale

Name_____

Date_____

Money Management Style Scale
Directions

Money management can be a difficult life skill for teens to acquire. Everyone has a different way, or style, of managing money. This scale will help you identify your money management style and then learn some techniques for more effective money management.

The scale contains 40 statements. Read each of the statements and decide to what extent the statement describes you. For each of the statements listed, circle the number of your response on the line to the right of each statement.

In the following example, the circled 2 indicates that the statement is a little like the person taking the assessment:

	A Lot Like Me	A Little Like Me	Not Like Me
Style 1:			
I buy whatever makes me happy	3	(2)	1

This is not a test and there are no right or wrong answers. Do not spend too much time thinking about your answers. Your initial response will likely be the most true for you. Be sure to respond to every statement.

(Turn to the next page and begin)

© 2013 WHOLE PERSON ASSOCIATES, 101 WEST 2ND ST., SUITE 203, DULUTH MN 55802 ▪ 800-247-6789

Money Management Style Scale

	A Lot Like Me	A Little Like Me	Not Like Me
STYLE 1			
I buy whatever makes me happy	3	2	1
I often buy gifts for other people	3	2	1
I have a hard time prioritizing what to buy	3	2	1
It is difficult for me to save money	3	2	1
I buy things on impulse	3	2	1
I often overspend the money I have	3	2	1
I often owe others money	3	2	1
I am not afraid to spend all the money I have	3	2	1
No gift is priced too high for me	3	2	1
I get a thrill from buying things	3	2	1

Style 1 - TOTAL = _____

	A Lot Like Me	A Little Like Me	Not Like Me
STYLE 2			
I like to hold onto my money	3	2	1
I am great at saving money	3	2	1
I have a plan for saving money and I stick to it	3	2	1
I will not buy things I don't need	3	2	1
I think twice before I buy anything	3	2	1
I like to have money saved in case I need it	3	2	1
I like the security of having money in the bank	3	2	1
I usually pay cash for what I buy	3	2	1
I am rarely in credit-card debt	3	2	1
I try to save a certain amount of money each month	3	2	1

Style 2 - TOTAL = _____

(Continued on the next page)

Money Management Style Scale *(Continued)*

	A Lot Like Me	A Little Like Me	Not Like Me

STYLE 3

	A Lot Like Me	A Little Like Me	Not Like Me
I often worry about not having enough money	3	2	1
I feel like it is up to me to control my spending	3	2	1
I often check to see how much I have saved.	3	2	1
I often think about what might happen to my money	3	2	1
I like to save for a rainy day	3	2	1
I worry that I will not have enough for what I need	3	2	1
I like my money to grow safely in a bank account	3	2	1
I like to be able to put my hands on my money easily	3	2	1
I worry when I buy something that costs a lot	3	2	1
I worry about money a lot.	3	2	1

Style 3 - TOTAL = _____

	A Lot Like Me	A Little Like Me	Not Like Me

STYLE 4

	A Lot Like Me	A Little Like Me	Not Like Me
I believe that people should pay for things I want	3	2	1
I don't care if my parents have to sacrifice	3	2	1
It's a parent's obligation to buy what a child wants	3	2	1
I never admit to making mistakes when I spend my money.	3	2	1
I expect to be given money regardless of what I do	3	2	1
I think my family owes me as much money as I need.	3	2	1
I don't think I should have to work to get nice clothes	3	2	1
I think my family should give me money when I ask for it	3	2	1
If I want something, someone should give it to me	3	2	1
I feel entitled to be given money until I can earn my own	3	2	1

Style 4 - TOTAL = _____

(Go to the Scoring Directions on the next page)

Money Management Style Scale
Scoring Directions

Teens often have a difficult time managing their money. The assessment you just completed is designed to measure your money management style. Add the numbers you've circled for each of the four sections on the previous pages. Put that total on the line marked TOTAL at the end of each section.

Transfer your totals for each of the four sections to the lines below:

Style 1: Spenders Total = _____

Style 2: Savers Total = _____

Style 3: Conscientious Manager Total = _____

Style 4: Entitlement Total = _____

Profile Interpretation

Individual Scales Scores	Result	Indications
Scores from 24 to 30	high	Scores from 24 to 30 on any single scale indicate that you have many of the characteristics of people with that money-management style.
Scores from 17 to 23	moderate	Scores from 17 to 23 on any single scale indicate that you have some of the characteristics of people with that money-management style.
Scores from 10 to 16	low	Scores from 10 to 16 on any single scale indicate that you do not have many of the characteristics of people with that money-management style.

Go to the next page to learn more about the various money-management styles.

For scales which you scored in the **Moderate** or **High** range, find the descriptions on the pages that follow. Then, read the description and complete the exercises that are included. No matter how you scored, low, moderate or high, you will benefit from **every one of these exercises**.

In the following exercises, remember to use Name Codes for the people you describe.

Money Management Style Scale
Profile Descriptions

For each of the styles, place a check in the box by the characteristics that sound like you.

STYLE 1: SPENDERS

As a Spender, you may get carried away by your need for instant gratification. You may feel compelled to spend or charge money very easily and quickly, even if you can't afford the purchases. Shopping provides you with psychological comfort and distraction. You may buy things you do not even need, but it is the act of shopping and spending money that satisfies you. You also like to keep up with what other teens wear and own. You may have many credit cards and many of them may be charged to their limit. You might feel like your debts are out of control, but find it difficult to stop seeking for the high you get from shopping and spending money.

Characteristics:

❏ You overspend to feel better about yourself.

❏ Shopping is a form of happiness for you.

❏ You often justify, especially to yourself, that other people have these things and why shouldn't you?

❏ You feel happier when you purchase material things.

❏ When you are having a bad day, you feel better by going shopping.

STYLE 2: SAVERS

As a Saver, you tend to be very financially stable. You feel a sense of pride in how you have earned and now manage your money. You focus primarily on feeling financially secure, and doing what you need to do to stay that way. You probably do not owe money and all of the choices you make are designed to keep it that way. You frequently check your total money situation in order to feel economically secure.

Characteristics:

❏ When it comes to money you are organized and focused on stability.

❏ You tend to be educated about money.

❏ You have conservative spending habits.

❏ You save to be sure you have money when you need it.

❏ You believe that the way to financial security is through saving.

(Continued on the next page)

Money Management Style Scale
Profile Descriptions *(Continued)*

STYLE 3: CONSCIENTIOUS MANAGER

As a Conscientious Manager, you may believe that the only way to feel financially secure is to hang on to every penny you earn. You may continually worry about money, and often let your anxiety get in the way of having fun. You may even feel like a problem may come up and you want to be ready. You prefer thrift over spending and are frugal, and you are willing to do without things you want. You are afraid of losing your money and you want to be prepared.

Characteristics:

- ❑ You build a stash of money that you can fall back on in case of an emergency.
- ❑ You like living on a budget.
- ❑ You like using coupons to save money when you shop.
- ❑ You are disciplined about money and are interested in advertisements and sales of necessary products.
- ❑ You live well within your means.

STYLE 4: ENTITLEMENT

As an Entitlement Manager, you feel like you are entitled to money. You feel that receiving money is a right and that you expect to receive your fair share. You don't worry about sacrifices that others have to make to supply you with money, you simply feel as if you deserve it just for being you. You often feel like you should receive money even if you do not work for it. You will most often look to other people to provide you with money when you need it.

Characteristics:

- ❑ You probably expect to receive money from others when you need it.
- ❑ You want to receive money even if you don't work for it.
- ❑ You feel entitled to have money.
- ❑ You expect others to pay for what you need and want.
- ❑ You feel like people should give you money for being you.

My Weekly Income

In the spaces that follow, list your sources of income: (use name codes)

Income Source	Where do you receive this money?	Weekly Income
Job		$
Allowance		$
Home Chores		$
Gifts		$
Other		$
Other		$
TOTAL		**$**

As you look at these figures, what surprises you?_____

_____

_____

_____

Do you need more money than you are receiving weekly and for what?_____

_____

_____

How you make do on this amount of money?_____

_____

_____

_____

What can you do to EARN more money? _____

_____

_____

_____

How I Spend My Money

This activity is designed to help you determine the approximate amount of money you are currently spending on a monthly basis. List the item and the amount of money you spend on it weekly.

Expenses

I. Entertainment

Ex: Saturday movie – $10 ticket and popcorn

_____

_____

_____

_____

_____

_____

II. Car

Ex: Gasoline $20.00 a week

_____

_____

_____

_____

_____

_____

III. Personal Needs

Ex: Drug store items – $13

_____

_____

_____

_____

_____

_____

(Continued on the next page)

How I Spend My Money *(Continued)*

IV. School Needs

Ex: School supplies $8 _____

_____

_____

_____

_____

_____

_____

V. Technology

Ex: iPhone $23 _____

_____

_____

_____

_____

_____

_____

VI. Other

_____

_____

_____

_____

_____

_____

_____

_____

_____

_____

Is it a Need or a Want?

This exercise will help you determine what you NEEEEEED and what you WANT. You can then determine what you can afford. (use name codes)

Items	Need & why	Want & why	What can I afford?	How will I do this?
Ex: Car	Car – so I can get a job		Gasoline, Insurance and a car payment after I get my job	XYZ pay for the down payment and I pay back with my wages
Car				
Clothing				
Technology				
Travel				
Entertainment				
Other				
Other				

© 2013 WHOLE PERSON ASSOCIATES, 101 WEST 2ND ST., SUITE 203, DULUTH MN 55802 ▪ 800-247-6789

My Money History

It is often helpful to look at how money was handled in your family when you were growing up:

What are your parents' or caregiver's thoughts about money management? (use name codes)

_____

_____

_____

_____

_____

_____

_____

How does the location of where you live affect your family's money management style? (use name codes)

_____

_____

_____

_____

_____

_____

_____

How financially comfortable is your family and how has this affected your current thoughts about money? (use name codes)

_____

_____

_____

_____

_____

_____

_____

(Continued on the next page)

My Money History *(Continued)*

Who takes care of the money management process in your house? Explain. (use name codes)

_____

_____

_____

_____

_____

_____

_____

_____

How frequently is money a discussion topic in your family? Why? (use name codes)

_____

_____

_____

_____

_____

_____

_____

_____

_____

How can you manage your money more effectively in the future?

_____

_____

_____

_____

_____

_____

_____

_____

Spending Habits

How are your money spending and saving habits similar to, or different from those of your parents/guardians? (use name codes) _____

_____

_____

_____

_____

How does the way your parents manage their money affect you (positively or negatively)? (use name codes)_____

_____

_____

_____

_____

If you overspend, do you attempt to hide your tendency to overspend? Explain. _____

_____

_____

_____

_____

How often do you spend more in a month than you have? On what do you overspend? How can you fix this situation?_____

_____

_____

_____

_____

In what ways does your spending and saving habits cause conflict between you and your family and friends? (use name codes) _____

_____

_____

_____

_____

(Continued on the next page)

Spending Habits *(Continued)*

What would you like to buy, but you have not done so because you cannot afford it?

_____

_____

_____

What things did you buy that you don't use or need?

_____

_____

_____

What are you concerned about that is money-related? (use name codes)

_____

_____

_____

What would you like to have, that you cannot afford, and no one will buy for you?
Why won't they? (use name codes)

_____

_____

_____

What can you do to be able to afford it? (legal!)

_____

_____

_____

If your life, or the life of your family, has someone suffered because you spend money on things you cannot afford – or – do *not* spend money on things you *can* afford. Explain. (use name codes)

_____

_____

_____

_____

_____

New Spending Behavior

How would you like to change your own spending behaviors?

_____

_____

_____

_____

_____

_____

How do you wish the person or people with whom you live would change their spending behavior? (use name codes)

_____

_____

_____

_____

_____

_____

_____

_____

_____

What would you like to buy but can't afford?

_____

_____

_____

How can you make some money and save it till you can afford to buy what you want?

_____

_____

_____

_____

_____

_____

_____

Money Quotations

Journal your thoughts about both the quotations below.

After a visit to the beach, it's hard to believe that we live in a material world.

~ Pam Shaw

_____

_____

_____

_____

_____

_____

_____

_____

_____

_____

The real measure of your wealth is how much you'd be worth if you lost all your money.

~ Author Unknown

_____

_____

_____

_____

_____

_____

_____

_____

_____

_____

_____

Money Management Definitions

401(k) Plan – A qualified retirement plan through an employer to which eligible employees can make salary deferral (salary reduction) contributions on a post-tax and/or pretax basis.

APR – Annual Percentage Rate. The annual cost of a loan; including all fees and interest. Expressed as a percentage.

Asset – Any resource that has economic value that an individual or corporation owns, opposed to liabilities.

Cap – The highest amount you have to pay on a loan.

Cash Flow – One of the main indications of a company's overall financial health. Calculated by subtracting cash payments from cash receipts over a period of time (month, quarter, year).

Compound Interest – Interest that is calculated not just on the initial principal but also on the accumulated interest from previous periods. As interest is added back to the principal, the rate of return applies to the entire balance, making the balance grow even faster than simple interest (simple interest is when the interest is applied only the initial principal, not the accumulated interest as well).

Credit Report – A summary of a person's credit history, showing historical information such as bankruptcies, loans, late payments, and recent inquiries. Individuals can obtain one free credit report from each of the three credit bureaus each year.

Credit Score – A measure of credit risk that is based on activities such as credit use and late payments.

Debt – An amount owed to a person or corporation for funds borrowed.

Inflation – The gradual increase or rise in the price of goods of a period of time.

Interest – The fee paid for using other people's money. For the borrower, it is the cost of using other people's money. For the lender, it is the income from renting the money.

Liabilities – Moneys owed, opposed to assets.

Loan – An agreement in which a lender gives a borrower money, expecting to be paid back.

Mortgage – A loan to finance the purchase of real estate, usually with specified payment periods and interest rates.

Net worth – Basic calculation of assets minus liabilities. Used both for corporations and individuals to measure financial health.

Principal – The original investment on which interest is generally paid.

Stock – A proportional share of ownership of a corporation. If a corporation offered 100 shares of stock and if you purchased 10, you have 10% ownership in it.

Scholarship – An award of financial aid for students to further their education. Scholarship money is not expected to be repaid.

What Don't You Know About Money?

Check the items that you do NOT know or understand.

- ❑ How taxes work and when you become responsible for paying taxes.
- ❑ How to establish credit and what are credit scores.
- ❑ How to balance a checkbook.
- ❑ How to save money.
- ❑ How and where to invest money.
- ❑ How credit cards work and what is interest.
- ❑ Basic banking.
- ❑ How to develop a budget.
- ❑ The connection between allowances and responsibilities.
- ❑ How to afford further education (government and personal loans, grants, scholarships, etc.)
- ❑ How to save for special occasions.
- ❑ How to guard against identity theft.
- ❑ How to determine the safety of online purchases.

Who is a person you know who is financially savvy?

1._____

2._____

3._____

4._____

5. _____

Put a star by the names of the people you listed above whom you can ask about the boxes you checked. Make a commitment to do this by _____ .

DATE

_____   _____

SIGNATURE   TODAY'S DATE

Money Management Tips

- Be aware of your money management style and work on improving it.

- Make a list of what you want to purchase and stick to it when you go to the store.

- If you use a credit card, use only one, and pay the total balance off each month so you are not paying interest.

- Have a budget and stick to it.

- Don't feel like you need to purchase the newest, latest electronic device.

- Find an inexpensive hobby to rely on when the urge to spend occurs.

- Avoid shopping when you feel anxious, angry or depressed.

- Ask yourself why you need to buy the latest styles to keep up with your peers.

- Find healthy ways to meet your need to spend. Giving to a charity will help someone else and can make you feel a lot better than spending it on something that will be out of style in a few months.

- Find ways to have a good time without spending a lot of money.

SECTION III:

Time-Management Skills Scale

Name_____

Date_____

Time-Management Skills Scale
Directions

Because you are probably busy with school, family, friends, work, volunteering and extra activities, it is critical that you learn responsible time management skills. People who are good managers of time tend to have successful study and work habits, and satisfying relationships. For others who are *managed-by-time* opposed to being time-managers, time brings anxiety, stress, frustration, exhaustion and complication. As a busy teen, you probably feel that you have too much to do and not enough time to do it. In this fast-paced society, learning how to manage your time can help you to alleviate stress and reduce anxiety in your life.

If you are struggling with time management, you're not alone. Many adults feel that there is not enough time in the day and that they need to learn effective time management skills. By learning better time management skills, you can regain control over your hours in each day. Rather than getting bogged down and not getting enough done, time management helps you to choose what you need to do and when to do it.

This assessment contains 32 statements that are related to your time management skills. Read each of the statements and decide whether or not the statement describes you. If the statement does describe you, circle the number in the YES column next to that item. If the statement does not describe you, circle the number in the NO column next to that item.

In the following example, the circled number under "Yes" indicates the statement is descriptive of the person completing the inventory.

	YES	NO
1. I have specific school goals	(2)	1

This is not a test and there are no right or wrong answers. Do not spend too much time thinking about your answers. Your initial response will likely be the most true for you. Be sure to respond to every statement.

(Turn to the next page and begin)

Time-Management Skills Scale

	YES	NO
GOAL SETTING		
1. I have specific school goals	2	1
2. I rarely write down my plans for the future	1	2
3. I prioritize my goals to decide what to work on next	2	1
4. I stress out about deadlines	1	2
5. I often say "yes" to things and then I wish I hadn't	1	2
6. Before I take on a task, I make sure the results are worth the time	2	1
7. I often set too many goals and then haven't the time to reach them	1	2
8. I take on more obligations than I have time to complete	1	2

TOTAL = _____

	YES	NO
PRIORITIZING		
9. I hang on to mail and emails even though I know they are unimportant	1	2
10. I work on tasks starting with those I decide are most important	2	1
11. I know how much time a project will take me	2	1
12. I analyze new tasks for their importance and then prioritize them	2	1
13. I keep a prioritized "to do" list	2	1
14. I talk to my friends and family about the priorities of tasks I am given	2	1
15. I hate to ask others for help in completing tasks, even if they are due	1	2
16. I work on projects that will yield the best results	2	1

TOTAL = _____

(Continued on the next page)

Time-Management Skills Scale *(Continued)*

	YES	NO

PROCRASTINATING

	YES	NO
17. I put off the things I don't like to do until the last minute 1		2
18. I put off tasks/assignments that may be too difficult 1		2
19. I often put things off because I don't know how to do them 1		2
20. I have trouble meeting deadlines set for me 1		2
21. I take pride in the fact that I usually complete tasks at the last minute 1		2
22. I return texts and emails immediately 2		1
23. I rarely have to ask for more time to complete an assignment 2		1
24. I often don't get my schoolwork done on time 1		2

TOTAL = _____

	YES	NO

SCHEDULING

	YES	NO
25. People say that I "have no sense of time" 1		2
26. I often overload my schedule with too many activities 1		2
27. I have a place I keep important papers 2		1
28. I set time aside to plan my work/school work 2		1
29. I create a 'to-do' list regularly for new tasks 2		1
30. I have time built into my schedule to deal with unexpected events 2		1
31. I don't wear a watch and don't pay attention to the time 2		1
32. I am often late 1		2

TOTAL = _____

(Go to the Scoring Directions on the next page)

Time-Management Skills Scale
Scoring Directions

Add each of the four columns and write the numbers in the blank spaces below.

GOAL SETTING   =   _____

PRIORITIZING   =   _____

PROCRASTINATING   =   _____

SCHEDULING   =   _____

Profile Interpretation

Individual Scales Scores	Result	Indications
Scores from 14 to 16	high	You tend to have excellent time-management skills in this area.
Scores from 11 to 13	moderate	You tend to have some time-management skills; there is room for you to improve as a manager-of-time.
Scores from 8 to 10	low	You tend to have limited time-management skills in this area. You seem to be managed-by-time rather than being a time-manager. You need to do as much as possible to improve your time management skills for personal growth.

Read the following descriptions on the next page and complete the exercises that are included. Regardless of how you scored on each of the scales, you will benefit from these time-management exercises.

Time-Management Skills Scale
Profile Descriptions

GOAL SETTING

Those who score low on this scale are not setting adequate goals. Once you have set goals, you can then know where you are going and what needs to be done to get there. With poor goal setting, you tend to spend your time on conflicting priorities. By setting goals, you will save yourself time, effort and frustration in the future. You need to begin setting concrete attainable goals and the steps needed to accomplish these goals on how you use your time.

PRIORITIZING

Those who score low on this scale need to work on prioritizing what needs to be done. Prioritizing helps you to work on those projects that are most critical. You need to develop a system for prioritizing and adding structure to your work. To work effectively, you need to work on the tasks that have the highest value and importance first.

AVOID PROCRASTINATING

Those who score low on this scale need to work on getting tasks done on time and not wait until the last minute. You need to develop the habit of not procrastinating or else tasks will back up until you are unable to complete them all. You might feel like you will put things off until you are rested or that you work best when under pressure. Pressure from undone tasks can cause stress in your life that is avoidable. Procrastinators often develop excuses to not get the task at hand completed.

SCHEDULING

Those who score low on this scale do not work on keeping a time schedule. You need to begin creating a schedule that can help to keep you on track and protect you from procrastination and the stress that goes with it. Develop an awareness of the factors that may be interfering with your ability to complete your work. Scheduling will ensure that you work on priority tasks and allow for unexpected events and interruptions.

A combination of these four skills creates a person
who is most effective in managing time.

Goal-Setting

Step 1 – Define Your Goals

It is important for you to determine what you would like to see happen in the future. This will help to give order and content to your daily schedule. This might include such things as being more efficient at work, getting involved with more community activities, or spending more quality time with your family. These types of goals will provide you with direction and priorities. You will need to give time and energy to the goals you develop for yourself.

The first step in setting and reaching your goals is to define them so they are realistic and measurable. Take a look at some sample goals:

Volunteer at an animal shelter	*Make a lot of money*	*Find a job*
Be accepted to a state college in fall	*Buy a new bicycle*	*Buy a car*
Get an A in math	*Have a date for the prom*	*Travel*

Notice that these goals are vague and difficult to measure. When you are developing goals for time management, remember that the goals should have the following characteristics: they need to be **SMART**: **S**pecific, **M**easurable, **A**ttainable, **R**elevant to you, and tied to a **T**imeline. Let's take a look at each of these characteristics in more detail:

- **Specific:** Goals must be stated in clear and definite terms. For example, *I would like to apply for and be accepted to a state college in fall* would be a clear and definite goal.

- **Measurable:** Goals must be measurable so that you can track your progress. For example, apply for and be accepted to a state college in the fall can be measured, while go to college is hard to measure.

- **Attainable:** Goals must be within your reach or you will not be motivated to work toward them. You must feel like you have a realistic opportunity to achieve your goals. For example, feeling like having the grades, motivation, finances, and resources to apply for and be accepted to a state college may not be realistic, whereas applying for and being accepted to a community college may be a viable option.

- **Relevant:** Goals must be important to you. For example, knowing that going to college will greatly enhance your career options, the amount of money you make, and the life you will live makes this goal very relevant to you.

- **Timeline:** Goals must have deadlines attached to them if they are going to motivate you, though you need to be reasonable and set deadlines that you can realistically commit to. For example, by stating that you would like to apply for State College by March 1 will help you keep committed to attaining that goal.

(Continued on the next page)

Goal-Setting: Step 1 – Define Your Goals *(Continued)*

Define your own goals. They should be positively stated and realistic, identify specific behaviors, and within your ability to achieve. Use the space below to set four or more goals that will help you live better in each of the following areas of your life. (use name codes)

My Personal Goals

_____   _____

_____   _____

My School Goals

_____   _____

_____   _____

My Relationship Goals

_____   _____

_____   _____

My Career, Job or Volunteer Goals

_____   _____

_____   _____

GOAL-SETTING: Step 2 – Prioritize Your Goals

The next step is to prioritize your goals into long-term and short-term by importance. Short-term goals are objectives that you would like to achieve in a year or less. These goals may be changed or revised as new options present themselves. Long-term goals are objectives that you want to achieve over a longer period of time, and can be set five to ten years into the future. Try to clarify what is urgent, what is somewhat important, and what can wait.

Use the space below to prioritize your goals into long-range and short-range goals. Be sure to place the short-term goals first. These may be related to your personal life, your family life, or your career. (use name codes)

Short-Term Goals *(Example: Get an A in math this semester)*

_____

_____

_____

Long-Term Goals *(Example: Go to a college)*

_____

_____

_____

GOAL-SETTING: Step 3 – Don't Procrastinate

Procrastination is the thief of time. Procrastination means that you put off things that you need to do or want to do until a later time. You may have trouble starting to work on your goals, or you may have trouble finishing a goal because you get distracted or begin working on another goal.

Answer the following questions to help you identify what you procrastinate about: (use name codes)

1. Think about something you have always wanted to do, but have put off. What is it?

_____

_____

2. What is keeping you from doing it? What are you avoiding?

_____

_____

3. Answer the question: "What is the worst thing that could happen if I do it?"

_____

_____

4. Identify a time when you can start to work on this goal:

   Day of the week _____   Time _____

5. When will you achieve this goal?

_____

Use the worksheet below to identify ways that you are procrastinating: (use name codes)

Reasons I procrastinate	What I am afraid of
Ex: I'm a perfectionist	"I'm afraid that I will not be as good as others and they will laugh at me."
I might make a mistake	
I'm worried about a confrontation	
I have feelings of being overwhelmed	
(Write your own reason here)	

GOAL-SETTING: Step 4 – Schedule Your Time

Scheduling is the process of allocating time for prioritized goals. It is planning time to accomplish individual goals. Strive to provide a set time schedule to achieve goals rather than having it imposed by people or conditions outside of you. For example, if your teacher gives you an assignment on Monday to read and research something by Friday, set your own goal of Thursday to have it finished. (use name codes)

Scheduling Techniques:

1. Time Blocking – Time Blocking is setting aside (or blocking out) a certain amount of time each day to spend toward accomplishing one of your goals. When would you like to block out time during your day?

   _____

   _____

2. What large goal do you have that you would like to break down into smaller goals?

   _____

   _____

   _____

   _____

3. Break this task into smaller (easier to accomplish) goals. List the smaller goals.

   _____

   _____

   _____

   _____

   _____

   _____

   _____

   _____

   . . . And how might this plan look?

   _____

   _____

   _____

   _____

   _____

   _____

   _____

Other Time Management Techniques

To-Do Lists

To-do lists are lists of things you want or need to do. This list will help you remember what needs to be done and not trust them to your memory alone. In this activity, you develop a list of things to be accomplished and when. As you complete items on the to-do list, you just check them off the list. Below, create a list of what you need or want to complete. (use name codes)

To do	When ?	Done
Ex: Get a summer part-time job	By May 15th	✔

Have More Time

What activity can you can spend less time with or stop doing completely in order to have more time for important matters? (use name codes)

What types of things can you do to have more time?

Part of my life	What I will do
Personal Time	*(Ex: Set a time limit for computer games)*
Relationship Time (Friends, Girl/Boyfriends, Family)	*(Ex: Check my texts every half an hour, not constantly)*
School Time	*(Ex: Quit some of the extra activities I am involved with)*
Work or Volunteering	*(Ex: Cut back on hours if I can't get necessities finished)*

Being More Assertive

Be assertive when you need to be. Time is a valuable commodity. Remember that it is your time and does not belong to other people. You may need to be more assertive in protecting the time you need and not allow people to steal time away from you. List the people who steal time from you and how they do this.
(use name codes)

People who 'steal' time from me	How they do it	What can I say or do?
Friend, BHY	She constantly calls me to talk about her boyfriend.	Tell her I have 5 (or 10) minutes to talk and then I need to go.

Managing Perfectionistic Behaviors

Perfectionism is the notion that you must complete each task perfectly (with no mistakes).

Are you a perfectionist? What makes you think so?

_____

_____

In what areas of your life are you a perfectionist?

_____

_____

How does that perfectionism take away your time?

_____

_____

Asking for Help

When you think about it, there will always be more to do than time to do it in. What activities or tasks do you do that steal a lot of your time? How can you ask others for help? (use name codes)

This Part of My Life	Who Can Help? (Name Code)	How Can This Person Help Me?
Ex: School	*MME*	*She can quiz me to help me get ready for a test.*
School		
Family		
Personal		
Friends		
Work or Volunteering		
Other		

Maintaining Balance in Life

When tasks become stressful, it is usually because you are experiencing an imbalance among the various roles in your life. Think about the amount of time you spend on your personal life, family, school, work, volunteering, leisure time and relationships. It is important to develop an awareness of what is most important and how much time you are spending. In this chart, think of a typical day and choose from the activities below or list your own in the appropriate time slot.

(Examples: alone time, care for others, cell phone, community activities, computer, eat, electronic games, email, exercise, family time, friends, hobbies, homework, household chores, movies, personal time, play, read, school, school clubs and extra activities, sleep, socialize, sports, television, texting, volunteer, work, etc.)

24 – Hour Time Frame	How I Spend My Time . . .
7:00 am – 8:00 am	
8:00 am – 9:00 am	
9:00 am – 10:00 am	
10:00 am – 11:00 am	
11:00 am – 12:00 Noon	
12:00 Noon – 1:00 pm	
1:00 pm – 2:00 pm	
2:00 pm – 3:00 pm	
3:00 pm – 4:00 pm	
4:00 pm – 5:00 pm	
5:00 pm – 6:00 pm	
6:00 pm – 7:00 pm	
7:00 pm – 8:00 pm	
8:00 pm – 9:00 pm	
9:00 pm – 10:00 pm	
10:00 pm – 11:00 pm	
11:00 pm – Midnight	
Midnight – 1:00 am	
1:00 am – 2:00 am	
2:00 am – 3:00 am	
3:00 am – 4:00 am	
4:00 am – 5:00 am	
5:00 am – 6:00 am	
6:00 am – 7:00 am	

Maintain Balance

In this second chart, identify how you can spend your time each day in ways that would work better for you. List the activities on the chart and the amount of time to spend on a typical day on that activity.

(Examples: alone time, care for others, cell phone, community activities, computer, eat, electronic games, email, exercise, family time, friends, hobbies, homework, household chores, movies, personal time, play, read, school, school clubs and extra activities, sleep, socialize, sports, television, texting, volunteer, work, etc.)

24 – Hour Time Frame	How I Spend My Time . . .
7:00 am – 8:00 am	
8:00 am – 9:00 am	
9:00 am – 10:00 am	
10:00 am – 11:00 am	
11:00 am – 12:00 Noon	
12:00 Noon – 1:00 pm	
1:00 pm – 2:00 pm	
2:00 pm – 3:00 pm	
3:00 pm – 4:00 pm	
4:00 pm – 5:00 pm	
5:00 pm – 6:00 pm	
6:00 pm – 7:00 pm	
7:00 pm – 8:00 pm	
8:00 pm – 9:00 pm	
9:00 pm – 10:00 pm	
10:00 pm – 11:00 pm	
11:00 pm – Midnight	
Midnight – 1:00 am	
1:00 am – 2:00 am	
2:00 am – 3:00 am	
3:00 am – 4:00 am	
4:00 am – 5:00 am	
5:00 am – 6:00 am	
6:00 am – 7:00 am	

Time Management Background

How does your family and extended family members manage their time? (use name codes)

_____

_____

_____

_____

_____

_____

_____

_____

_____

_____

_____

How has that background affected your sense of time? Do you manage time as they do or differently? How?

_____

_____

_____

_____

_____

_____

_____

_____

_____

_____

_____

My Time Management

In what parts of your life do you already manage time well?

_____

_____

_____

_____

_____

_____

_____

_____

_____

_____

In what parts of your life do you want to improve your time management?

_____

_____

_____

_____

_____

_____

_____

_____

_____

_____

_____

_____

Uh Oh! You're Late!

> **Better three hours too soon, than one minute too late**
>
> ~ William Shakespeare

Are you a punctual person? _____

Do you get to your dates, school or appointments on time? _____

Are you the person who always comes in late and disturbs whatever is happening? _____

Can people depend on you? _____

If you are often late, why? _____

_____

_____

Being on time can make a huge difference on how people view you!

- You make a good impression on people.
- You earn a reputation of being someone others can count on.
- You demonstrate integrity.
- You show efficiency and dedication.
- You display dependability
- You seem organized and in control.
- You give people the feeling that they can trust you.
- You do not appear rude when you are on time. Instead, you appear respectful.

What can you do to prevent being late?

- Mark down every appointment and the time you need to be there on a calendar or to-do list – check it often!
- Rehearse what you need to say if you're with someone and need to go. *I hate to cut you off, but I need to leave now. I have an appointment.*
- Assume that everything takes longer than you think. If it takes you 10 minutes to get to work, leave 15 or 20 minutes early. You can always read a book, talk with someone, or text or phone someone.
- When someone asks you for something right before you are leaving to go somewhere and you feel can't say no, say, *I would love to help, but I'm on a deadline* or *I need to be at work in half an hour. I can help you tomorrow.*
- Set an alarm clock or your cell phone alarm to remind you to get up or to keep certain appointments.

Punctuality breeds credibility!

Time Management Tips

- Eat healthy and have enough sleep.

- Focus your energy on the most important tasks.

- Organize homework.

- Improve productivity at school.

- Limit after school activities, if needed.

- Create good study habits.

- Keep a prioritized To-Do list with you at all times and use it.

- Create a schedule.

- Develop a routine and stick with it.

- Set long and short-term goals and complete them.

- Accomplish what needs to be done calmly, with less stress and anxiety.

- Find a healthy balance between friends, family, school, work, volunteering and recreation.

- Choose carefully. Do not say yes to every opportunity.

- Avoid people who steal time from you.

- Make time for extras you really want to do.

- Always volunteer some time in your week to help someone.

- Stay focused on the task.

SECTION IV:

Self-Awareness Scale

Name_____

Date_____

Self-Awareness Scale
Directions

Self-awareness is the recognition of your emotions and their effects (emotional awareness), knowledge of your strengths and limits (self-knowledge), and sureness about your self-worth and capabilities (self-confidence). The Self-Awareness Scale can help you identify your own self-awareness by exploring these three areas.

This assessment contains thirty statements. Read each of the statements and decide if the statement is true or false. If it is true, circle the word **True** next to the statement. If the statement is false, circle the word **False** next to the statement. Ignore the numbers after the True and False choices. They are for scoring purposes and will be used later. Complete all thirty items before scoring this scale.

In the following example, the circled False indicates that the item is false for the participant completing the scale:

EMOTIONAL AWARENESS

1. I am able to understand and acknowledge my feelings. . . . True (1) (False (0)) Score_____

This is not a test and there are no right or wrong answers. Do not spend too much time thinking about your answers. Your initial response will be the most true for you.
Be sure to respond to every statement.

(Turn to the next page and begin)

Self-Awareness Scale

EMOTIONAL AWARENESS

1. I am able to understand and acknowledge my feelings . . . . True (1) False (0) Score_____

2. I do not withhold my feelings. . . . . True (1) False (0) Score_____

3. I understand how my feelings affect other people . . . . True (1) False (0) Score_____

4. I sometimes get too emotional . . . . True (0) False (1) Score_____

5. My emotions often negatively affect my actions. . . . . True (0) False (1) Score_____

6. I know which emotions I am feeling . . . . True (1) False (0) Score_____

7. I understand the link between my emotions
   and what I think . . . . True (1) False (0) Score_____

8. My emotions often help me to better understand situations True (1) False (0) Score_____

9. I cannot change my emotions. . . . . True (0) False (1) Score_____

10. It is important for me to understand my emotions . . . . True (1) False (0) Score_____

TOTAL _____

SELF-KNOWLEDGE

11. I know which things I don't do well . . . . True (1) False (0) Score_____

12. I have a good sense of humor . . . . True (1) False (0) Score_____

13. I do not like to think critically about what happens
    in my life. . . . . True (0) False (1) Score_____

14. I like to learn new things . . . . True (1) False (0) Score_____

15. I am open to feedback from others . . . . True (1) False (0) Score_____

16. I can describe my strengths . . . . True (1) False (0) Score_____

17. I can describe areas where I need to improve. . . . . True (1) False (0) Score_____

18. Learning and growing is not important to me right now . . . True (0) False (1) Score_____

19. I like to receive different opinions from other people. . . . . True (1) False (0) Score_____

20. I learn from my experience and do not make
    the same mistakes . . . . True (1) False (0) Score_____

TOTAL _____

(Continued on the next page)

Self-Awareness Scale *(Continued)*

SELF-CONFIDENCE

21. I believe that I am talented . . . . True (1) False (0) Score_____

22. Others say I have a great personality . . . . True (1) False (0) Score_____

23. I like myself . . . . True (1) False (0) Score_____

24. My abilities compare favorably with the abilities
    of others. . . . . True (1) False (0) Score_____

25. I am easily overwhelmed . . . . True (0) False (1) Score_____

26. I go out on a limb for what is right. . . . . True (1) False (0) Score_____

27. I have trouble making decisions under pressure . . . . True (0) False (1) Score_____

28. I am very self-confident . . . . True (1) False (0) Score_____

29. I am okay to voice views that may be unpopular
    with my peers. . . . . True (1) False (0) Score_____

30. I speak out about injustices in the world . . . . True (1) False (0) Score_____

TOTAL _____

(Go to the Scoring Directions on the next page)

Self-Awareness Scale
Scoring Directions

The Self-Awareness Scale is designed to help you to better understand yourself.

To score the Self-Awareness Scale total your score for each section and then transfer them to each of the individual scales below.

Emotional Awareness Scale: Total Score from #1 through #10 = _____

Self-Knowledge Scale: Total Score from #11 through #20 = _____

Self-Confidence Scale: Total Score from #21 through #30 = _____

Profile Interpretation

Individual Scale Score	Result	Indications
0 to 3	low	On this scale, you do not score as being very self-aware. It is important for you to do everything you can to better understand your strengths and weaknesses.
4 to 7	moderate	You score somewhat self-aware on this scale. You can benefit from becoming even more self-aware.
8 to 10	high	You score self-aware on this scale. Continue to do everything you can to retain your self-awareness.

The higher your score on the Self-Awareness Scale, the more self-aware and emotionally tuned in you are. No matter if you scored in the **Low**, **Moderate** or **High** range, the exercises and activities that follow are designed to help you learn to increase your self-awareness even more.

Profile Descriptions

EMOTIONAL AWARENESS

People scoring high on this scale are able to quickly and easily recognize the emotions they are feeling and understand the effects that these emotions have on their thinking and actions. They rely on their ability to focus and know the subtle internal signals that tell them what they are feeling. They are able to manage their negative feelings, keep themselves motivated, and accurately tune in to the feelings of those around them. They are able to develop and use good social skills and build long-term relationships with other trusted people.

SELF-KNOWLEDGE

People scoring high on this scale are able to quickly and easily know and understand both their strengths and weaknesses, work to improve their weaknesses, work continuously toward greater self-development, and learn from their experiences. They are interested in learning as much as possible about both positive and negative aspects of themselves. They are receptive to open, honest and direct messages from other people, and use these messages to improve themselves. They are aware of their limitations and know where they need to improve.

SELF-CONFIDENCE

People scoring high on this scale are aware of their own capabilities, values, and goals and have the presence and confidence to voice opinions that are different from those of other people. They have a likeable personality and inspire confidence in people around them. They are able to make tough decisions and follow a course of action they believe in. They believe in their abilities and will work hard to persist through difficulties. They believe in their skills and are able to effectively use the skills they have.

Emotional Awareness

Becoming aware of your emotions is not something that comes very easily. Part of the reason for this difficulty is that to tune into feelings, you must experience them. Negative emotions, such as sadness, anger, hate and guilt, can be very painful to experience and many people will tune them out or deny them. By doing so, you spare yourself the agony of feeling bad at the moment, but you prevent yourself from using the valuable information that these feelings can provide you. To get more in touch with your emotions, try some of the following:

Become more aware of the physical behaviors associated with your emotions.

Begin to pay attention to the outward signs of your emotions. Think about a time when you experienced a negative emotion (such as feeling embarrassed when you stood up to speak in front of a crowd). What did you experience physically (a red face, stomach in knots, feeling faint, etc.)?

What is a time recently when you felt a negative emotion? (use name codes)

_____

_____

_____

_____

_____

_____

_____

_____

What physical symptoms did you notice that were associated with the emotion?

_____

_____

_____

_____

_____

_____

_____

_____

My Feelings

For the next week, at a particular time each day, write the feelings you experienced during the preceding hours and the cause of those feelings. (use name codes)

Time/Day	Feelings	Cause
Ex: 7 a.m. Monday	Anxious about going to school	I didn't do my homework
Monday		
Tuesday		
Wednesday		
Thursday		
Friday		
Saturday		
Sunday		

(Continued on the next page)

My Feelings *(Continued)*

At the end of the week, review what you have written. Do you find that you experienced certain emotions more than others (anger, optimism, etc.)? What were these emotions? (use name codes)

_____

_____

_____

_____

_____

_____

_____

_____

What caused these emotions? Describe the causes.

_____

_____

_____

_____

_____

_____

_____

_____

What changes could you make to alleviate the negative emotions and experience more positive emotions?

_____

_____

_____

_____

_____

_____

_____

Self-Assessment

Self-assessment is learning as much as you possibly can about yourself and finding out what makes you unique. The following questions are designed to help you with this process. (use name codes)

What are your strengths?

_____

_____

_____

_____

_____

What would others say your strengths are?

_____

_____

_____

_____

_____

What are your areas for growth?

_____

_____

_____

_____

_____

What would others say are your areas for improvement?

_____

_____

_____

_____

_____

(Continued on the next page)

Self-Assessment (Continued)

How do your friends describe you?

_____

_____

_____

_____

In what ways do you agree with your friends' descriptions of you? (use name codes)
Explain your reactions.

_____

_____

_____

_____

In what ways do you disagree with your friends descriptions of you? (use name codes)
Explain your reactions.

_____

_____

_____

_____

What motivates you? Why?

_____

_____

_____

_____

Who motivates you? Why?

_____

_____

_____

_____

(Continued on the next page)

© 2013 WHOLE PERSON ASSOCIATES, 101 WEST 2ND ST., SUITE 203, DULUTH MN 55802 ▪ 800-247-6789

Self-Assessment *(Continued)*

What are your dreams for the future?

_____

_____

_____

What steps are you taking to achieve your dreams?

_____

_____

_____

What do you fear most in your life? Why?

_____

_____

_____

What stresses you?

_____

_____

_____

What is your typical response to stress?

_____

_____

_____

What qualities do you like to see in people? Why?

_____

_____

_____

Do you have many friends with the qualities you just described? (use name codes)

_____

_____

I Am Unique

Awareness is the first step in changing your life. ~ Michael Lee

In the table that follows, identify what makes you unique:

I am unique in the following roles	Ways I am unique
Ex: Family	*I am the first person in my family to go to college after high school.*
Family	
School	
Relationships	
Community Service	
Hobbies	
Work	
Other	

Self-Confidence

Self-confidence is the ability to see yourself realistically, capable, able and willing to take on any challenges and master new tasks or skills.

What would you like to do to change your future?

_____

_____

_____

_____

What new skills are you confident that you could learn?

_____

_____

_____

_____

What abilities do you possess that you are most confident about?

_____

_____

_____

_____

When you disagree with someone's viewpoint, what do you do?

_____

_____

_____

_____

What types of things would you stand up to other people?

_____

_____

_____

_____

My Strengths

To be more self-confident, you need to identify your strengths. In the table that follows, list those things you do well when you are working with your hands, working with ideas and creativity, working with numbers, and working with people. (use name codes)

When I work with . . .	I can . . .
Ex: My hands	*Play video games, fix computers*
My hands	
Ideas and creativity	
Numbers and data	
People	

My Present Areas for Growth

To be more self-confident, you also need to know your areas for growths and limitations. In the table that follows, list those things you would like to do better when you are working with your hands, working with ideas and creativity, working with numbers, and working with people. (use name codes)

When I work with . . .	I would like to . . .
Ex: My hands	*be able to fix my car when it breaks down*
My hands	
Ideas and creativity	
Numbers and data	
People	
Other	

Self-Awareness

Write five true statements about your characteristics and abilities beginning with the words _I am._

1. _I am_ _____

2. _I am_ _____

3. _I am_ _____

4. _I am_ _____

5. _I am_ _____

How did you decide what to write about?_____
_____
_____

How easy or difficult was it difficult to come up with 5 statements? _____
_____

Did you tell much about yourself?_____
_____

What did you learn about yourself?_____
_____
_____

What are three positive words you would use to describe yourself?

    1. _____

    2. _____

    3. _____

Why would you use these words to describe yourself? _____
_____
_____

My Dreams

How will being more self-aware help you reach your present dreams?

_____

_____

_____

_____

_____

_____

_____

_____

_____

_____

How will being more self-aware help you reach your dreams for your adult future?

_____

_____

_____

_____

_____

_____

_____

_____

_____

_____

_____

_____

Self-Awareness Quotations

- -

*"We judge ourselves by what we feel capable of doing,
while others judge us by what we have already done."*

~ Henry Wadsworth Longfellow

What do you feel you are capable of doing?

_____

_____

_____

_____

- -

*"Change occurs when one becomes what she is, not when
she tries to become what she is not."*

~ Ruth P. Freedman

What is an example of a time when you tried to become someone you are not?

_____

_____

_____

_____

- -

*"You can live a lifetime and, at the end of it, know more about other people
than you know about yourself."*

~ Beryl Markham

**Do you believe that could be true about yourself? If so, what can you do to
prevent it?**

_____

_____

_____

_____

- -

(Continued on the next page)

Self-Awareness Quotations *(Continued)*

- -

"Hide not your talents, they for use were made. What's a sundial in the shade?"

~ Benjamin Franklin

What talents do you have that you do not use? How can you start using them?

_____

_____

_____

_____

- -

For a long time, the only time I felt beautiful – in the sense of being complete as a woman, as a human being, and even female – was when I was singing."

~ Leontyne Price

What talents or skills do you have that allow you to feel complete?

_____

_____

_____

_____

- -

"I've learned to take time for myself and to treat myself with a great deal of love and respect . . . cause I like me. I think I'm kind of cool."

~ Whoopi Goldberg

Do you think Whoopi would be just as successful as she is, if she didn't think she was cool? Explain.

_____

_____

_____

_____

_____

SECTION V:

Personal Change Scale

Name_____

Date_____

Personal Change Scale
Directions

Change is constant in the lives of people of any age. We need to do everything in our power to be accepting of change, realizing that things don't always stay the same, and making the best of the situation that we can.

The Personal Change Scale contains 32 statements that are related to changes that affect people. Read each of the statements and decide whether or not the statement describes you. If the statement is TRUE, circle the number next to that item under the "True" column. If the statement is FALSE, circle the number next to that item under the "FALSE" column.

In the following example, the circled number under "FALSE" indicates the statement is not true of the person completing the scale.

	TRUE	FALSE
I have experienced the following changes in the past year . . .		
(A) I changed schools 2		(1)

This is not a test and there are no right or wrong answers. Do not spend too much time thinking about your answers. Your initial response will likely be the most true for you. Be sure to respond to every statement.

(Turn to the next page and begin)

Personal Change Scale

	TRUE	FALSE

I have experienced the following changes in the past year . . .

	TRUE	FALSE
(A) I changed schools	2	1
(A) I dropped out of school	2	1
(A) I can't decide whether to further my education	2	1
(A) I have trouble maintaining good grades in school	2	1
(A) I used to like school and I hate it now	2	1
(A) I am having problems with teachers	2	1
(A) I set unrealistic expectations for myself in school	2	1
(A) I started skipping school	2	1
(B) My family moved	2	1
(B) I had to live with someone else	2	1
(B) One of my parents/caregivers was fired	2	1
(B) A family member experienced a health problem	2	1
(B) I have a new family	2	1
(B) My parents separated/divorced	2	1
(B) I experienced death of a family member or friend	2	1
(B) I have had trouble with siblings	2	1

(Continued on the next page)

Personal Change Scale *(Continued)*

	TRUE	FALSE

I have experienced the following changes in the past year . . .

	TRUE	FALSE
(C) I experienced an illness or injury	2	1
(C) I experienced a change in my looks	2	1
(C) I had legal troubles	2	1
(C) I started smoking/drinking alcohol	2	1
(C) I watched a person being bullied and didn't know what to do	2	1
(C) I disclosed an alternative lifestyle	2	1
(C) I made a major change that affected my future.	2	1
(C) I lost a close personal relationship.	2	1
(D) I have been bullied	2	1
(D) I have had to make new friends	2	1
(D) I was pressured to do something I knew was wrong	2	1
(D) I have started bullying others	2	1
(D) I have a new boyfriend/girlfriend	2	1
(D) I experienced dating violence	2	1
(D) I have been cyber stalked	2	1
(D) I joined a gang	2	1

(Go to the Scoring Directions on the next page)

Personal Change Scale Scoring Directions

This scale is designed to identify those areas in your life in which you have experienced change. To get your scores, total the numbers that you circled for the statements marked (A) in the previous section. You will get a number from 8 to 16. Put that number in the space marked "(A) – School Total" below. Then do the same for the other three scales – (B) – Family, (C) – Personal, and (D) – Peers.

(A) – SCHOOL TOTAL   =   _____

(B) – FAMILY TOTAL   =   _____

(C) – PERSONAL TOTAL   =   _____

(D) – PEERS TOTAL   =   _____

Profile Interpretation

Individual Scales Scores	Result	Indications
Scores from 14 to 16	high	You are experiencing a great many changes in that part of your life. Developing effective personal change management skills would be very important for you.
Scores from 11 to 13	moderate	You are experiencing some changes in that part of your life. You might need to develop some additional personal change management skills to deal effectively with current changes as well as future changes.
Scores from 8 to 10	low	Scores from 8 to 10 on any single scale indicates that you are not currently experiencing a lot of change in that part of your life at this time. Continue to develop effective personal change management skills in anticipation of changes that might occur in your life.

Scale Descriptions

Read the descriptions below and complete the exercises that are included in this scale. No matter how you scored, low, moderate or high, you will benefit from these exercises.

(A) – SCHOOL — People scoring high on this scale are experiencing stressful changes in their lives at school and in making educational decisions.

(B) – FAMILY — People scoring high on this scale are experiencing stressful changes in their family lives.

(C) – PERSONAL — People scoring high on this scale are experiencing stressful changes in their personal lives.

(D) – PEERS — People scoring high on this scale are experiencing stressful changes in their relationships with their peers.

How Do You Respond to Change?

Change can affect your life. Write about a changes you are currently going through. (use name codes)

_____

How is this change affecting your body? (headaches, exhaustion, stomach problems, pain, etc.)

_____

_____

_____

How is it affecting your mind? (confusion, negative thoughts, forgetfulness, sleep, etc.)

_____

_____

_____

How is it affecting your feelings and emotions? (depression, anger, fear, frustration, etc.)

_____

_____

_____

How is it affecting your spirituality? (lack of commitment, purpose, meaning in life, etc.)

_____

_____

_____

By learning the signals, you will be able to take steps towards your transition. When things are changing in your life, you need to learn positive ways to manage yourself. Regardless of what is happening around you in your environment, you will always have control over how you respond to stress, what types of things you do, how you feel and what you think.

How Can I Cope?

A feeling of control over our life is one of the fundamental needs that all human beings have. During time of change and transition it is natural for you to feel out of control. That's when you begin to experience difficulties. You may feel helpless in your situation and unable to change things, or you might even feel like you are a victim and this is only happening to you. Either way, you get stuck on the idea that you are out of control of your own life. It is time to start thinking about ways that you can regain control over your situation and your life.

To increase your personal power over change in your life, you can do several things:

- Take care of yourself.
- Create a positive inner self.
- Create a strategy to take action.
- Deal with your changing situation and develop a support network to help you.

We will look at all four of these strategies individually.

Taking Care of Yourself

Staying in the Present

Much of the stress that you are experiencing comes from worrying about the changes in your life and how you will work to regain control over these changes. To reduce and ultimately stop worrying, you need to start living in the present moment. When you do this, all of your attention becomes focused on what you are currently doing.

Breathing

Because breath is vital to life itself, proper breathing is very important and can even be an excellent form of stress reduction related to change in your life. Diaphragmatic breathing, in which you take in long, very deep breaths, is an especially powerful tool for relaxation. To do this you push out your stomach and draw in a long deep breath. Then you exhale as slowly and as long as possible. Repeat this until you feel yourself relaxing.

Exercise

Exercise is another excellent method for combating and managing stress. The time needed to exercise is often hard to find, but it is very important that you put aside time in order to exercise your body and relieve tension.

Nutrition

Many people admit that during high stress periods they tend to eat more or eat less than usual. They also eat less healthy foods. A good diet contributes physically and mentally in a positive way.

Progressive Relaxation

Progressive relaxation helps you to bring relaxation to all parts of your body through concentrated awareness. It allows you to actually produce relaxation by focusing self-suggestions of warmth and relaxation in specific muscle groups throughout the body. Start with your toes and relax your way up to your head, or the other way around.

Interests

By continuing to participate in healthy activities that interest you, you can cope well with the stress associated with change.

Develop a Support Network

It is vital to have a supportive network of people who you can trust. Think of your support network as a team of people who can help you through this time of change. By discussing your problems, goals and dreams with these people, you can reach out to them and, in turn, you can help them when they are in need.

Create a Positive Inner Self

To increase your personal power over the change occurring in your life, draw on your inner resources. It is time to see yourself as capable, resourceful and a master of change. Complete the following chart to help you recognize your positive inner self. (use name codes)

My strengths	*Example: My ability to do well in math and the sciences.*
My skills and talents	*Example: I like and get along well with people of all ages.*
Resources I have available	*Example: MBB is always right there for me.*
Positive attitudes I possess	*Example: I always give people the benefit of the doubt.*
What I have to offer	*Example: I care.*

Self-Defeating Prophesies

Your inner beliefs and attitudes are important for you to be successful in managing change. When you continue to think pessimistic thoughts, they become self-fulfilling prophesies (a prediction or statement that directly or indirectly causes itself to come true), and then you fail to achieve success. Pessimistic thoughts can cause you to feel helpless and hopeless about the change that is occurring in your life.

Examples of these types of thoughts include:

I can't do this.   *I can't change anything in my life.*

The future will only get worse.   *I know I'm going to fail the test.*

If you are thinking those types of thoughts, you need to steer your attitude in a more positive direction. You need to begin using positive affirmations to help guide your thoughts and actions. Positive affirmations are phrases you can use to reprogram your mind to include more positive thoughts. They are brief statements that put you in the proper frame of mind to accept intuitive inputs. Affirmations are a way of sending your brain a message that the desired result has already been achieved. What you state, in the present tense, can easily be achieved. Examples of affirmations that might be used in helping to guide you through change ...

Change is inevitable. I can control my reaction to it.

Change can be an opportunity for me.

Life is changing fast, but I can do it.

I do have some control over the change in my life.

I am going to maintain a positive attitude towards this change in my life.

Create Your Own Affirmations

Using the examples of affirmations above, compose some of your own affirmations:

_____

_____

_____

_____

_____

To strengthen your coping skills in stressful situations, practice your affirmations on a daily basis. Select one of the affirmations that you feel comfortable with and repeat the affirmation for about five minutes each day for one week.

Regain Control

It is vital for you to be aware of what you have control over and what is not within your control as you work through a change that you are experiencing. The following exercise will help you with this process. (use name codes)

Think about the type of change you are currently experiencing. Describe it below.

_____

_____

_____

What emotions are brought out by this change? (i.e., scared, angry, happy, etc.)

_____

_____

_____

List the things that you **_cannot_** control in this situation.

_____

_____

_____

What types of information do you need to gain about this situation in order to have greater control?

_____

_____

_____

Now list the things that you **_can_** control in this situation.

_____

_____

_____

Now identify those things you can control, that you would like to focus on immediately.

_____

_____

_____

Create a Strategy to Take Action

Take Action

People who deal well with change are able to take an active, purposeful approach to change. They look for positive things that they can change and take action to do so.

Review the list of things you identified that you can control (in the last exercise you completed), and in the left column list those things. In the right column, explain how you will take action. (use name codes)

Things I Can Control	How I Will Take Action

Considering a Change

When you experience personal change, you need to be aware of the resources you possess and those that you lack. Answer the following questions to identify whether you are ready for a change. (use name codes)

What change would you like to make?_____

_____

_____

_____

_____

In what way is this change under your control? _____

_____

_____

_____

_____

If it is not, how can you make the best of it?_____

_____

_____

_____

_____

If this change is under your control, is this the best time? _____ If not, when would it be?

_____

_____

_____

_____

Who can you talk with to help you make decisions or advise you about this change?

_____

_____

_____

_____

(Continued on the next page)

Positive Thinking

It is important to continue to think positively as you proceed through the process of change. People often fall into the trap of allowing their negative thinking to keep them feeling down and depressed. Look at some of the following positive statements people will tell themselves in the midst of a change.

Everything will work out well.

Everyone experiences change.

I won't let this change disrupt my life.

I can turn this change into something positive.

I will take responsibility for how I feel, think, and act.

Change is a challenge to me.

Change can be positive.

Now you try. What are some positive thoughts you have about your change?

_____

_____

_____

_____

_____

_____

_____

_____

_____

_____

_____

_____

_____

_____

_____

_____

_____

What's the Worst that Could Happen?

Often times we exaggerate the severity of changes we are going through. We focus on the negatives and think about the worst things happening. Describe a change you are currently going through or are considering. (use name codes)

_____

_____

_____

How do you feel about the change?

_____

_____

_____

_____

What is the worst thing that could happen after the change and how would you handle it?

_____

_____

_____

_____

What are some of the more probable things that could happen?

_____

_____

_____

_____

What actions can you take to make sure the worst does not happen?

_____

_____

_____

_____

How Change Affects Me and Others in My Life

It is important to look at not only how a change you are considering will affect you, but also the other person or people involved. Think of changes in your life that happened and the effects.

The change	How I was affected	Who else was affected (name codes)	How others were affected
Example: We moved to another city.	I miss my friends. I feel lonely. It's hard to be the new kid in school.	MBB MBF MM	He had to find a job. She misses me. They had to find a house.

© 2013 WHOLE PERSON ASSOCIATES, 101 WEST 2ND ST., SUITE 203, DULUTH MN 55802 ▪ 800-247-6789

Me And Change

What things scare you most about change?

_____

_____

_____

_____

_____

_____

_____

_____

_____

_____

_____

What things excite you most about change?

_____

_____

_____

_____

_____

_____

_____

_____

_____

_____

_____

_____

Change Management

What techniques for change management do you like best?

_____

_____

_____

_____

_____

_____

_____

_____

_____

_____

_____

_____

What techniques for change management do you not feel comfortable with? Why?

_____

_____

_____

_____

_____

_____

_____

_____

_____

_____

_____

_____

_____

_____

Quotations ~ Change

Pick two of your favorite quotes and write about why you chose them.

We must learn to view change as a natural phenomenon – to anticipate it and plan for it. The future is ours to channel in the direction we want to go . . . we must continually ask ourselves, "What will happen if . . ." or better still, "How can we make it happen?"
~ **Lisa Taylor**

Very often a change of self is needed more than a change of scene.
~ **Arthur Christopher Benson**

Change is the process of becoming or making something different.
~ **Eric Komoroff**

Sometimes it's the smallest decisions that can change your life forever.
~ **Keri Russell**

_____
_____
_____
_____
_____
_____
_____
_____
_____
_____
_____
_____
_____
_____
_____
_____
_____

Changes in Teens

- Changes in thinking

- Changes to body

- Development of a self-concept

- Development of self-esteem

- Enhanced memory and cognitive processing

- Increase in hormones

- Increase in self-consciousness

- Increase in unhealthy risk-taking behaviors

- Increased attention span

- Independence

- Onset of identity development

- Peer Pressure

- Thoughts become more complex and abstract

- Development of mature relationships

Social Changes in Teens

- Changing role in family structure

- Increased need for autonomy

- Increase in parent/caregiver-teen conflicts

- Increase in romantic relationships

- Increase in time spent with peers

- Independent choices about food and fitness

- Influence from social media

- Influence of more than family members

- Selection and involvement in more adult leisure activities

wholeperson

Whole Person Associates is the leading publisher
of training resources for professionals who empower

people to create and maintain healthy lifestyles.
Our creative resources will help you work effectively with

your clients in the areas of stress management,
wellness promotion, mental health and life skills.

Please visit us at our web site: **www.wholeperson.com**.
You can check out our entire line of products,
place an order, request our print catalog, and
sign up for our monthly special notifications.

Whole Person Associates

Duluth MN 55802

800-247-6789